CONTENTS

√

CUBS: WHAT WILL YOUR NEXT CHALLENGE BE?

One of the great things about Scouting is the chance to take part in lots of different activities. Now you're a Cub Scout, there are even more things to try out. There are more adventures to be had, and more badges to work towards. So, why not try something new?

This book tells you everything you need to know about earning badges. They're your reward for being adventurous and taking part.

Whatever you decide to do, your leader and other adults can help you. That's why this book is in two sections:

- The first part is for you to read. We hope it's easy to understand. If anything's not clear, or there's a word in here you don't know, ask your leader or another adult.
- The second part has some things that adults will need to know. This is so they can help you earn your badges or awards.

If you see this symbol on the page, it means your leader will need to follow certain rules to make sure you're safe.

So when you're choosing a badge to go for, make sure you look though this book together with your leader or another adult who is helping you.

CORE
BADGES

BE PREPARED...

Core badges

Being part of your Pack is fun and it's something
you can be proud of. And guess what?
You can earn badges for taking part in the
Cub programme.

MEMBERSHIP AWARD

This award helps you understand your Promise and your commitment when you become a Cub Scout. It is presented to you at your Investiture ceremony.

How to earn your badge

1. Find out about the Cub Pack:
- Get to know the other members and leaders in your Six and Pack.
- Find out about the ceremonies and traditions in your Pack.
- Find out about the activities that your Pack does.

2. Find out about joining your Pack:
- Learn and understand the Cub Scout Promise and Law. Find out what the rules are in your Pack.
- Learn and understand the Cub Scout Motto, Sign, Salute and Handshake.
- Find out what to do at your Investiture.
- Find out the meanings of the badges you will receive. (Reading this book helps!)
- Show that you know about the family of Scouts, worldwide Scouting and the history of Scouting.

3. Become a Cub Scout by making the Promise.

Top tips

It's best to do steps 1 and 2 before you make your Promise and receive your badge.

JOINING IN AWARD

These badges celebrate your commitment to Scouting. It's also for taking an active part in Cubs.

How to earn your badge

The badges are numbered, so you can be awarded a new badge every 12 months from your very first day in Scouting. If you were a member in another section, the badge numbers carry on from the ones you already have.

These badges aren't just for Cubs. They recognise how long you have been part of Scouting in total.

You can be awarded up to three Joining In Awards while you're a Cub.

MOVING ON AWARD (CUBS TO SCOUTS)

You can earn your Moving on Award when you move from Cubs to Scouts.

How to earn your badge

1. Go to both Cubs and Scouts for at least three weeks. Take part in the Troop programme.
2. Work for your Scout Membership Award at the same time.

ACTIVITY

BADGES

ACTIVITY BADGES

There are loads of activities you can take part in and earn badges for. Whether you like art or astronomy, surfing or street sports – you'll find something you really enjoy, for the fun and the challenge.

ANIMAL CARER

Pets and animals need a lot of care. Your Animal Carer badge will show everyone how well you look after your four-legged friends.

How to earn your badge
1. Choose one of these to do:
   - Take care of a pet for at least three months. Give it the correct foods, and learn to recognise common illnesses and how to treat them.
   - Help to care for a farm animal for at least three months. Know the correct foods to give it and be able to recognise common illnesses. Learn what special care you need to give before and after the birth of farm animals.
2. Then choose two of these to do:
   - Keep a record of bird, animal or insect life in your garden, local area or park. Keep pictures, sketches, photographs or audio recordings. Do this for at least three months.
   - Visit a zoo, wildlife park, animal sanctuary or rescue centre. Find out about some of the animals you see. What are their feeding habits and natural habitats?

- Belong to an animal, bird or wildlife society. Either take part in one of its activities or make progress in any award scheme it offers.
- Find out about dangers that threaten wildlife in their natural habitat. Make a poster, collage or drawing or tell other Cub Scouts what you found out.

ARTIST

Art gives you the chance to use your imagination and get creative with paints and pens. So why not get stuck in to a new project and work towards your Artist badge?

How to earn your badge
Choose three of these activities to do. You must have your leader or another adult with you for one of these activities.

- Imagine an event, character or scene. Now draw it using a pencil, brush, pen or crayon.
- Design and make a greetings card.
- Make a poster advertising Scouting or a Cub Scout event.
- Design and make a decorated book cover.
- Draw or paint a picture of still life or a landscape.

- Make a display of photographs on a subject that interests you.
- Make a video on a subject that interests you.
- Design and build a model.
- Visit an art gallery.
- Make a model out of clay.

Top tips
You can use a computer to make either the greetings card or the poster, but not both. A handmade card or poster might take a bit of effort, but it'll look great.

ASTRONOMER

Explore space and find out more about the planets, stars and systems beyond planet Earth. Your Astronomer badge will help you on your search beyond the stratosphere.

How to earn your badge
1. Make a model or draw a simple diagram of the Solar System.
2. Explain the difference between a planet and a star.
3. Learn how to observe the sun safely. Find out and explain how the earth moves around the sun.

4. Observe the moon, using binoculars or a telescope if you can. Describe some of its features.
5. Identify three constellations.
6. Find out about two space-related subjects. Present some information about them.

Top tips
Visit this BBC webpage for useful stuff about stargazing: **tiny.cc/s9yzmx**

For number 6, you could find out about: planets, comets, the Northern Lights, the sun, eclipses, meteorites, black holes, the moon, light years or space exploration.

ATHLETICS

Whether you're running, jumping or taking on the egg and spoon race, this badge is about trying your best. Athletics is great because you try and improve as you practice.

How to earn your badge

1. Take part in a proper warm up and warm down routine, using all the main muscle groups. A suitable adult, Young Leader or Scout will need to lead the routine.
2. Explain the best clothes to wear for athletics and how to be safe.
3. Take part in one of these throwing activities:
   - Throw a tennis or cricket ball as far you can. Do one overarm throw and another underarm throw.
   - Throw three beanbags into a bucket. Try to increase the distance each time.
   - Throw a football or similar ball as far as you can. Do one using a chest push and another as an overhead throw.
4. Take part in two of these running activities and try your best:
   - shuttle run 6 x 10m
   - 50m skip with a rope

- 50m sprint
- 25m sack race
- 25m egg and spoon race
- 400m run.

5. Take part in one of these team activities:
   - 4 x 100m relay
   - team assault course
   - assisted blindfold race.

6. Do one of these jumps and go as far or as high as you can:
   - sargent jump
   - standing jump
   - high jump
   - long jump.

Top tips
Your leader will award you the Athletics badge for taking part and doing your best. Take this chance to see how well you can do!

For number 1, your routine might involve: skipping, running on the spot, stretching both arms high above your head and then relaxing down, bending your knees and dropping your head, rolling your head slowly around, and tensing and relaxing the shoulders.

You could gain the Athletics badge by taking part in a sports day in your Pack or the District, so long as it includes the activities we've listed.

For the high jump, you must be very careful about the way you jump. You also need special equipment and crash mats for your landing. You must not try to do the Fosbury Flop unless you've been taught how to do it properly and an expert is there to watch you.

ATHLETICS PLUS

Do you want to try and do even better in athletics? If you already hold the Athletics badge you can go for the next step and aim higher.

How to earn your badge

Take part in all the activities on the table. Take your best four scores and, if the points you score add up to eight or more, you get your badge.

Events	You get 3 points for	You get 2 points for	You get 1 point for
50m sprint	9 seconds	10 seconds	11 seconds
Throwing a cricket ball	25 metres	22 metres	18 metres
High jump	96cm	86cm	76cm
Long jump	3 metres	2.5 metres	2 metres
Sargent jump	35cm	30cm	25cm
Shuttle run 6 x 10 metres	18 seconds	19 seconds	20 seconds
50m skip with a rope	12 seconds	13 seconds	14 seconds
1,000 metre run	5 minutes	6 minutes	10 minutes

For the high jump, you must be very careful about the way you jump. You also need special equipment and crash mats for your landing. You must not try to do the Fosbury Flop unless you've been taught how to do it properly and an expert is there to watch you.

Top tips

For the sergeant jump, the person checking your score will get you to stand straight against the measure, with your arm stretched up. They will then adjust the measure so it starts from the tips of your fingers. The measurements depend on how high you can hit the measure with a jump. There are videos online that show how it's done.

For the shuttle run, the limits of the run will be marked on the ground. To finish the run, your hand or foot must touch on, or past, the mark.

BACKWOODS COOKING

Making something warm and tasty to eat takes a lot of skill, especially on a campfire. Impress everyone and find out how to make a hot meal at camp.

How to earn your badge

1. Show how to light a fire.
2. Help someone prepare a fire for cooking on.
3. Cook something using a billy can.
4. Cook something in the embers of a fire.
5. Cook something on a stick.
6. Show how to make the fire safe when you have finished with it. Extinguish the fire and make the area safe.

BOOK READER

It's great to get into a good story or book. So if you read a lot, why not show it by working towards the Book Reader badge?

How to earn your badge

1. Make a list of at least six books you have read or used recently. Books you have read on an e-reader count too.
2. Name the authors of your books. Tell your leader or other Cubs something about three of your books. At least one book should be fiction and one should be non-fiction.
3. Show that you know how to care for your books.
4. Show that you can use a dictionary and a thesaurus. You can use printed ones or online versions.
5. Explain to a leader how the books in a library are set out. How you would find fiction and non-fiction books?

CHEF

Could you whip up a tasty meal, using healthy ingredients? Get ready to tickle those tastebuds…

How to earn your badge

1. Learn the basic rules of safety and hygiene in the kitchen. Explain why they're important.
2. Talk to your leader about the different ways of preparing and cooking food.
3. Learn what the major food groups are. How do they fit into a healthy diet?
4. Plan, cook, serve and clear away a two-course meal for at least two people. You should prepare and cook vegetables as part of the menu. Remember, an adult must supervise you for this step. Talk to the people you're cooking for about the menu.

COLLECTOR

Certain objects tell us a lot about people, places and history. Why not go for this badge and build up a collection of things that interest you?

How to earn your badge

1. Over three months, build up a collection of similar items. It could be anything, like stamps, coins, postcards or fossils.
2. Display your collection in an exciting and interesting way.
3. Talk about items in your collection. Which things particularly interest you?
4. View a collection made by someone else. What do you like or dislike about the way it's presented?

COMMUNICATOR

Learn about different ways to communicate – whether you want to decode a secret message or reach lots of people at once.

How to earn your badge

1. Get someone to give you directions or instructions to do something. Check that you have understood. Then follow the directions or instructions.

2. Get someone you know to give you a call. Write down what they say, making sure that you have all the main details.

3. Show you can send emails and text messages. You could also show how to use a mobile phone or a tablet to send a message to someone.

4. Introduce yourself to an adult who helps out with your Pack. Talk to them for two minutes about your life, school or hobbies.

5. Choose three of these activities to do:

   • Report on a local event, either past or present. It could be written for something like a newsletter or recorded so people can listen to it.

   • Make contact with another Pack. Send them videos, letters or emails for whatever length of time your leader suggests.

- Find out how people with a visual or hearing impairment communicate. You might learn about Braille, Makaton or British Sign Language. Learn a simple phrase in one of the ways you have learned.
- Tell a story about an experience you've shared with your leaders and other Cubs. Make sure that you communicate clearly and that everyone is following the story.
- Hold a simple conversation in another language.
- Write three simple messages using codes, ciphers, invisible ink or semaphore. Try to work out three similar messages given to you.
- Get an adult or Young Leader to give you a message. Remember it and repeat it back to them 10 minutes later.
- Pass a message to someone using amateur radio.
- Take part in Jamboree On The Air (JOTA) or Jamboree On The Internet (JOTI).

CYCLIST

It's good to know how to care for and ride your bike well. The more you look after it, the more you can get out on it.

If you've gained Bikeability Level 2, you automatically get this badge.

If you haven't, there are two parts to earning your Cyclist badge.

First, do all five of these tasks.
1. Regularly use a bicycle, which is the right size for you, with a cycle helmet.
2. Show you can clean and oil a bicycle. Show how to pump up the tyres and mend a puncture.
3. Explain why you must lock up a bicycle when you leave it unattended.
4. Make a poster to promote road safety to pedestrians or cyclists.
5. Talk to your leader or other Cubs about the safety measures you need to take when you cycle in bad weather.

Next, choose one of the two options. Finish all the tasks for the option you choose.

Option 1

- Show that you can mount and dismount your bike properly.
- Show how to keep your bicycle in a roadworthy condition. Why is it important?
- Explain why it's important to use lights and reflective clothing.
- Go for a short ride in a safe place to show an adult that you can ride safely and confidently.

Option 2

- Find out about the safety equipment you need for cycling off-road.
- Show that you're able to control your bike over different types of terrain.
- Find out where, in your local area, is safe to cycle off-road.
- Plan and carry out a five-mile cycle ride off-road.

! You must always wear a cycle helmet when riding your bike. The only exception is if you're Sikh and you wear a turban.

DISABILITY AWARENESS

Sometimes people need different kinds of support to take part in activities. You can help by finding out about disability.

How to earn your badge

Choose one thing to do from each of the four lists.

1. Disability awareness
   - Explain what a disability is. What are the different types of disability?
   - Research a famous person with a disability. Make a poster or write about their life and achievements.
   - Visit a local community building like a library, town hall or cinema. How accessible is it for someone with a disability? Write down what you find out.
   - Show how you could help someone with a disability to make the Cub Promise. Think of a different example to the ones in steps 2, 3 or 4.

2. Physical disability awareness
   - Find out about two different aids that can assist a disabled person. How do they help? You could find out about things like wheelchairs, computers, rising chairs or adapted cars.

- Find out about three ways to make it easier for a wheelchair user to use public places, like shops, parks, hospitals or libraries. How could your meeting place be made better for a wheelchair user?
- Make a sandwich using only one hand or draw a picture using only your feet to hold the pen.

3. Deaf awareness
- Learn the alphabet using fingerspelling. Show you understand a word communicated to you using fingerspelling.
- Learn a song in Makaton or British Sign Language.
- Explain what equipment a deaf person might use in the home. You might look at special features on things like fire alarms, telephones or TVs.
- Show how you would approach a deaf person and speak to them so they can lip-read.

4. Sight awareness
- Describe two different ways a blind or visually impaired person can read. You could talk about how they would use computers, Braille or Moon.
- Explain what guide dogs for blind people do. How are they trained?
- Learn and read your name in Braille.
- Show how to approach a blind or visually impaired person. How would you identify yourself?

Top tips
There are lots of websites that can tell you about
different disabilities. We've included some on page
146 in the section for adults helping you.

DIY

Hammer, hang, sand and stain,
make nice things for your home –
or repair them again!

How to earn your badge
1. Show how to use and take care of tools safely.
   Do this for a selection of them, like a hammer,
   saw, screwdriver, drill or glue gun.
2. Talk to your leader about how to work safely
   on your projects, especially when you're using
   electric tools.
3. Learn what the difference is between hard
   wood, soft wood, chipboard, plywood and MDF.
   For each of them, find out what they're best
   used for.
4. Help design and make two items while an adult
   supervises you. Use them to show that you're
   able to:
   • measure accurately
   • saw

- join pieces of wood together in two different ways
- use a hammer, screwdriver and drill
- prepare surfaces and stain, varnish or paint.

Top tips
Your projects for number 4 might include:
- nesting box
- window box
- toolbox
- pencil box
- key rack
- mug tree
- coat rack
- bookends
- bookstand.

ENTERTAINER

With a little planning and confidence you can put on a fantastic show. Now, get ready for super stardom…

How to earn your badge
Choose two activities from the list to do.
- Help to make up a mime or play, then perform it.

- Perform a puppet play or shadowgraph using puppets that you have made.
- Help to plan and perform some recorded entertainment, like a video or audio story.
- Sing two songs.
- Perform some folk or traditional dances.
- Make a selection of simple rhythm instruments. Use them in a music performance.
- Tell a story to an audience.
- Make up and perform a dance to a piece of music of your choice.
- Help plan and perform a series of magic tricks.
- Take part in a show, concert or band performance.

ENVIRONMENTAL CONSERVATION

Do you care about the environment? With a bit of effort and coordination, you can help make sure it's looked after for years to come.

How to earn your badge

1. Learn how to separate recyclable and non-recyclable rubbish ready for collection. Find out where to take recyclable items that cannot be collected with your normal rubbish.

2. Find out how to reduce the energy and water you use in your home. Show how you have encouraged your family to reduce water and energy use over four weeks.

3. Find out about one type of renewable energy. Talk to your leader about the advantages and disadvantages of the technology.

4. Take part in two projects with a group of other people. You could:
   - clear a ditch, pond or creek
   - make, set up and look after a bird feeder, table, nesting box or bath
   - look after a piece of land or a garden
   - tidy up a piece of wasteland
   - take part in an anti-litter campaign
   - plant a tree or shrub
   - look after a compost bin.

Top tips
For number two, you could use a smart meter to track the change in your home energy use.

EQUESTRIAN

Saddle up and get ready to ride! Show off your skills in horse riding and learn how to take care of your trusty steed.

How to earn your badge

1. Show that you know how to dress safely for riding. Explain why it's important to wear a hard hat and the proper footwear.
2. Point out the main body parts of a pony or horse.
3. Point out the main parts of a saddle and bridle.
4. Learn how to approach a pony or horse correctly.
5. Learn how to mount and dismount a horse safely.
6. Show the correct way to sit in the saddle.
7. Show how to hold the reins correctly.
8. Show how to walk and trot safely in an enclosed area, without a leading rein.
9. Show you can do two of these skills:
   • walking without stirrups
   • walking on a loose rein and shortening the reins
   • riding up and down a hill at walking pace
   • cantering
   • riding over a single pole or very small fence.

FIRE SAFETY

Fire can spread very quickly. If you know what to do when a fire starts it can make a big difference.

How to earn your badge

1. Choose one of these activities to do:
   - Visit a fire station or invite a fire fighter to your meeting place.
   - Learn about some of the other things that fire fighters do. How do they help in road traffic accidents, rescuing people or animals, fitting smoke detectors and safety inspections at homes, schools or offices?
2. Take part in a fire drill at your meeting place. What should you do if a fire breaks out?
3. Make an emergency escape plan for your home.
4. Find out why it's important to use smoke and heat detectors. How would you check they're working and change their batteries?
5. Point out three possible dangers at home or your meeting place that could start a fire.
6. Find out how to keep a campfire safe for everyone. How do you stay safe around a fire?
7. Explain how you should behave around a bonfire and fireworks.

GLOBAL ISSUES

Being a Cub is about helping other people and there are no limits to how far your help could go. In fact, you can help other people in communities across the world.

How to earn your badge

1. Draw the logos of three to five international charities. Find out about what they do and why.
2. Find out how much energy you use in your meeting place or home. Over two weeks, record what energy you use forthings like lights, heating or cooking. Make a plan to reduce the amount of energy you use and put it into action.
3. Take part in an international awareness day or week.
4. Use pictures to show what you would need to survive if you became homeless because of a disaster, like flooding or an earthquake.
5. Identify five belongings of yours that have come from other countries. Point out the countries on a map. Talk to others about why your belongings have come from so far away.

Top tips

For number 3, you might take part in something like World Aids Day, World Water Day, International Day of Friendship or International Week of Science and Peace. You can find more on the United Nations website **un.org/en/events/observances/days**

There are lots of international charities. Save the Children, Oxfam, Operation Smile and Shelterbox are just some of them. Search online to find more.

HOBBIES

If you have a hobby and you want to develop it, why not go for this badge? It's perfect if your hobby isn't covered by one of the other badges.

How to earn your badge

1. Learn the safety rules for your hobby, if there are any.
2. Show that you're interested in your hobby and that you're taking part regularly for at least three months.
3. Show your leader, or other Cubs, how you pursue your hobby. Show what equipment, materials and background information you have used.

4. Talk to your leader about how you plan to develop your hobby, interest or skill in the future.

HOME HELP

Being helpful around the home will really impress your parents or carers. And when you grow up and live in your own house one day, you'll know exactly what to do.

How to earn your badge
1. Plan, cook and serve a simple one-course meal.
2. Wash up afterwards. Show how to clean a saucepan or other cooking utensils, cutlery and glasses. You could use a dishwasher for this step, including loading and unloading it.
3. Help sort out the washing. Load and unload the washing machine.
4. Iron at least two items. They could be things like pillowcases, t-shirts or trousers.
5. Sew on a button.
6. Help to clean and tidy a living room.
7. Clean at least two items in your home. They could be things like a basin or kitchen cupboard, silverware or brass.
8. Take sheets, pillow covers and the duvet cover off a bed and help to put clean ones on. Make your own bed for a week.

HOME SAFETY

Everyone should feel safe at home. You can help by preventing accidents and knowing what to do when they happen.

How to earn your badge
1. Find out what to do about a burst water pipe, gas leak or electricity power failure in your home.
2. Identify the common causes of accidents in the home. How can they be prevented?
3. Find out how to protect your home from crime.
4. Find out where the nearest public telephone box is to your house. Where else could you make an emergency call if the public telephone wasn't working?
5. Make a list of useful emergency numbers.

INTERNATIONAL

Would you like to explore the world? Kickstart your international adventure by getting to know other countries and cultures.

How to earn your badge

1. Draw or create the World Scout Badge. Explain the meanings of each of its parts.
2. Create a passport with information about a country. You could include things like its currency, national dress, foods, religions, cultures, customs and languages.
3. Cook a traditional dish from another country using an ingredient that you are not familiar with. Tell your leader what you liked or disliked about it.
4. Take part in the activities of a celebration or festival that usually takes place in another country. Explore why the celebration or festival happens. What are the customs of the event?

Top tips

For number 4, you could visit a festival or hold a celebration as part of a Pack evening or Scouting event. Festivals like Mela, Holi, Mardi Gras and Chinese New Year are good examples

LOCAL KNOWLEDGE

Do you know where to go in your local area? What about important places and history in your town?

How to earn your badge
Do three of the activities on this list.

1. Find out about a famous person who lived in or near your area. The famous person could be from the past or present. Or you could learn about a famous building, monument, earthworks or other place of historical interest and visit it. Talk about what you find out with your leader or other Cubs.

2. Collect pictures of your county, borough, district, town or village coat of arms. Find out what the coat of arms represents. Try to find as many different places as you can where the coat of arms is displayed. Tell your leader how many you found.

3. Talk to someone who has lived in your local area for a long time. Find out about what life was like when they were young. What changes have they seen in the local area over the years?

4. Draw a map of your area. Mark places of interest on it and, with other Cubs, go on a short walk in your local area. Point out any features of interest to your leader.

5. Design a poster, leaflet or web page to advertise your area to a visitor.

MARTIAL ARTS

Martial arts is a pretty cool hobby. But not only that, it teaches you to be confident, self-disciplined and healthy.

How to earn your badge
1. Regularly take part in a martial arts activity for at least three months. Show how you've improved over that time. Your martial arts activity should be recognised by your nation's sports council.
2. Discuss with a leader the skills needed and the rules to be observed.
3. Take part in one exhibition or competition.

Top tips
Martial arts activities include aikido, judo, ju jitsu, karate, kendo, sombo, taekwondo, tang soo do and wrestling. Here are the different sports councils for each nation:
- Sport England **sportengland.org**
- Sport Scotland **sportscotland.org.uk**
- Sport Wales **sportwales.org.uk**
- Sport Northern Ireland **sportni.net**

MY FAITH

If you have a faith, you can enjoy finding out more about it and thinking about what it means to you.

How to earn your badge

1. Find out about your place of worship and something about:
   - the people involved, their titles and what they do
   - the important or sacred objects
   - the festivals and customs
   - the stories and traditions. These could be from books, videos or other places.

2. Choose a favourite prayer or reading. You could even write the prayer yourself. Share it with the Pack at a time that's good for everyone. Explain to the Pack why you like it and what it means to you.

3. Choose your favourite festival. Explain what it celebrates or means and talk about the food, clothes and customs associated with the festival.

NATURALIST

Do you love wildlife and being outside? Find out about the natural environment and how to protect it.

How to earn your badge
1. Learn how to identify six different living things from two of these categories:
   - trees
   - garden birds
   - water birds
   - minibeasts and insects
   - wild flowers
   - pond dwellers
   - fungi
   - butterflies and moths.

   That means you should have 12 examples in total.
2. Over three months, visit the same natural area at least four times. Take a note of the changes in the plants and wildlife that you see. You might visit a garden, hedgerow, canal, river lake or park. Make sure that you have an adult's permission for the visits.
3. Learn the countryside code and how to follow it.

4. Choose one of these activities to do:
- Create a piece of art using natural material. You could do a bark or leaf rubbing, dried flower picture or maybe a collage.
- Use a dye that uses natural ingredients to colour a piece of material.
- Make a feeding station for birds. Get permission to hang it in a good position.
- Make a hedgehog, ladybird or bee house.
- With an adult pick wild edible berries, leaves or fruit. Use them in a recipe.

❶ For number 2, an adult has to say it's OK for you to go and visit a natural area. They must know where you are and how long you are going to be.

If you're picking plants or berries for number 4, make sure you are 100% sure you know what it is and whether it's safe to eat. If you're not sure, don't eat it.

Top tips
There are websites that can help you identify edible wild plants. Some even give you recipes for them. Try visiting **countrylovers.co.uk/wfs**

PERSONAL SAFETY

When you're out and about, taking part in adventures, keeping yourself safe is a must.

How to earn your badge

1. Explain the dangers of playing on or near two of these:
   - railways
   - busy roads
   - building sites
   - cliffs
   - canal banks
   - sand
   - gravel pits
   - farmyards
   - river banks
   - quarries
   - moorlands
   - lakes.

2. Show you can use at least one of these codes:
   - Water Safety Code
   - Bathing Code
   - Firework Code.

3. Make up a safety code of your own choice. It could be for car passengers, train passengers or the playground.

4. Explain what you must do if a stranger starts to talk to you. What must you tell your parents or carers if you are going out without them?
5. Find out how and why you might contact a helpline like ChildLine, for example.
6. Explain the best ways to stay safe while online. Write down some common sense rules to follow while you are on the internet.
7. Memorise your address and your home telephone number or a parent's mobile phone number.

PHOTOGRAPHER

Learn to capture some amazing images of people and places, and hang them proudly on your wall.

How to earn your badge
1. Show that you know how to use and look after your digital camera. Show how to turn it on and off, use the zoom function, charge or replace the batteries, insert a memory card and transfer pictures from the camera to a computer or tablet.
2. Take at least five photographs of local landmarks that could be used to make a tourist leaflet.

3. Take photos while you're on a visit, Pack outing or camp. Present 10 of your best pictures to someone else after the event. You could present them in a scrapbook, on a screen, in a photo book or some other way.
4. Choose one of these activities to do:
   - Take two pictures of the same thing – one in colour and one in black and white. Compare how the effects change the way the final picture looks.
   - Using a digital camera, make a short film on a subject of your choice.
   - Using a series of photographs, make a short animation sequence.
   - Take a photo of people, animals, an urban scene or a landscape. Think about the light, the positioning and setting of your photo. Explain why you composed your photo in the way that you did.

Top tips
You could use one of these tools to make your short film or animation sequence:
- Windows Movie Maker
- Microsoft PowerPoint
- iStopMotion for iPad
- SloPro
- Vine
- Instagram
- iMovie for Mac and iOS.

PHYSICAL RECREATION

Are you into sports and games? Here's your chance to get more involved and take part in a sport or physical activity that interests you.

How to earn your badge

1. Show a good sporting attitude in all games and sports you take part in.
2. Tell your leader about the sports you take part in. Find out as much as you can about your sports, especially the rules.
3. Show that you're fairly skilled in your sports. Take part for three months or more in at least one of your chosen sports.
4. Bring the clothing and equipment for the sport you've chosen along to a meeting. Show how to look after them.
5. Tell a leader about the training and preparation you take part in for your chosen sport. How and when do you practise?

PIONEER

With pioneering skills, you
can work together to build
something great.

This is what you need to do to earn your badge.
1. Make your own rope, perhaps using a rope
   machine or working with a friend.
2. Tie a simple lashing.
3. Show how you would:
   • tie three different knots, such as a reef, figure
     of eight, sheet bend or bowline
   • make one hitch, such as a clove hitch, round
     turn and two half-hitches or a cow hitch.
4. Take part in a knot game.
5. Build an indoor pioneering project using simple
   knots and lashings.

Top tips
Your leader will be able to find knot games
and activities involving making rope on
scouts.org.uk/pol

ROAD SAFETY

Using the roads is part of everyday life, especially if you want to get out and explore. So staying safe on the roads is essential.

This is what you need to do to earn your badge.
1. Draw or take photos of 10 different traffic signs. Explain what they mean.
2. Show how to use the Green Cross Code.
3. Tell a leader why it's important to have different types of pedestrian crossing. Explain how to use them safely.
4. Show that you know how to behave safely as a car passenger

SCIENTIST

From animals to minerals to travelling through the air – we use science to find out about the universe around us. So pop on your safety goggles and get experimenting.

How to earn your badge
Do six activities. You should choose at least one from each of these sections.

For each one, explain or show to a leader what you did and what you found out.

Section 1: reactions

- Show how vinegar reacts with different items and explain what happens. The different items could be steel wool, sodium bicarbonate or old dirty coins.
- Find out what happens when you add salt to water.
- Compare the density of water to the density of other liquids. Show how these liquids react to each other.
- Make a pH indicator solution. Use it to test the acidity or alkalinity of other liquids.
- Grow crystals.

Section 2: interacting with energy

- Create a basic electrical circuit which includes a switch. Show how it could be used to control a lightbulb powered by a battery.
- Make an air powered balloon rocket or a water rocket. Investigate ways of improving how far it can travel.
- Make a simple compass. Show the effects of metallic and magnetic materials upon it.
- Use marshmallows and spaghetti to build the strongest tower you can. Explain how you have improved your design.
- Find a way to show that hot air rises.

Section 3: living things

- Set up a wormery or ant colony. Record what happens over three or four weeks
- Investigate what happens to your pulse rate before, during and after exercise.
- Grow cress, beans, peas or a similar plant. Investigate what happens when the plant has no access to light. What happens when it has light, but no water?
- Find a way to show that plants take water up through their stems.
- Make some yoghurt and find out how living organisms are involved in the process.

Top tips

It's fine if you'd like to do a different experiment which fits under one of the categories. Just get agreement from your leader.

SKATER

Find your balance and get confident on wheels or blades. You'll be skating effortlessly before you know it.

How to earn your badge
1. Use a skateboard – or in-line, quad or ice skates – for at least three months.
2. Learn some safety rules about skating on the road and in other public places. Show what clothing and protective equipment you need to wear for your activity. You might include helmets, knee pads or elbow pads.
3. Show how to start, stop and turn safely.
4. Show how to fall safely and regain balance.
5. Show how you do three different manoeuvres. You could demonstrate travelling backwards, spinning, jumping or turning.

SPORTS ENTHUSIAST

If you love sport but follow it rather than play it, show off your expert knowledge

How to earn your badge

1. Follow your chosen sport for at least three months.
2. Find out the rules and laws of the sport. Explain them to an adult.
3. Show you have a good knowledge of the teams and personalities in your chosen sport.
4. Explain what equipment is needed for the sport.
5. List some major events for the sport of your choice.
6. Describe events that you have attended for your chosen sport. If you haven't been to an event, explain to your leader how you keep up-to-date with your sport.

WATER ACTIVITIES

If you love to be in the water, whether you're wearing a snorkel or riding a wave, then this badge is definitely for you.

How to earn your badge
Earn your Water Activities badge in two parts. First, explain the safety rules for all water activities. Then choose one of these options.

Option 1
Reach one of these standards:
- British Sub Aqua Club's Dolphin Snorkeler Qualification
- Professional Association of Diving Instructors' Discover Scuba (Bubble Maker) or Seal Team Programme
- British Surfing Association's Junior Scheme Level One Award
- British Water Ski & Wakeboard's Cutting Edge Participation Certificate
- RYA Windsurfing Youth Stage 1.

Option 2
Take part in two of these activities:
- scuba diving
- snorkelling
- windsurfing

- water skiing
- surfing
- rafting.

Top tips
If you'd rather take part in a water activity that involves boating, why not try the Nautical Skills staged activity badges? You can find details on page 99.

WORLD FAITHS

Finding out about different religions and faiths can help you better understand different people and traditions.

How to earn your badge
1. Visit a place of worship which is important to one of the World religions. Find out some information about the building, what's inside it and how it's used for worship.
2. Meet someone who belongs to one or the World religions, or has a set of beliefs which are different to your own. Find out how they put their faith into practice.
3. Find out about the places of religious significance for a World religion.

4. Find out about the religious festivals and customs linked to a World religion.

ACTIVITY PLUS

Is there an activity you'd really like to take further? If you have the highest level of any of the badges in this book, the Activity Plus badge could be your next big challenge.

Your leader can award it if you have done really well in an activity. You can also earn the Activity Plus if you've taken something on even though you don't have the best facilities available.

How to earn your badge
To earn an Activity Plus badge you need to:
- hold your chosen activity badge
- agree a target with your leader before going for the Activity Plus badge. It might mean you have to take part in some more training or practice to help you learn more.
- show your leader that you have met your target.

Here are a few examples of targets for Cubs:

- For the Book Reader Plus, read at least another six books. Name the authors and tell your leader or other members of the Pack about them.
- For the Cyclist Plus, gain the Bikeability Level 3.
- For the DIY Plus, finish a DIY project that is more difficult than the example given.

The only activities that are not included in the Activity Plus are Athletics and Athletics Plus.

A PLUS badge can be awarded for any activity badge, apart from the following: Athletics, Athletics Plus, Community Impact, Hikes Away, Nights Away, Time on the Water. When an Activity PLUS is awarded for a staged Activity Badge it can only be awarded against the highest stage of that badge.

STAGED ACTIVITY BADGES

BE DETERMINED...

Staged activity badges give you the chance to try something new or get better at something you already know.

You can choose the right stage for your skills, rather than your age. With staged activities, you get to try the same challenges as Beavers, Scouts and Explorers. You can jump ahead to a higher stage if you're ready.

If you do stage 1 or stage 2, that's great too. In fact, most Cubs will do activities at these stages.

Talk to your leader about what's best for you.

AIR ACTIVITIES

How do aircraft work? How do you chart a journey across the sky? Investigate these and other interesting facts about flight

Now, get ready for take-off…

How to earn your badge
1. Make an aircraft out of paper. How well does it fly? You could use a paper dart or a helicopter and drop it from a height.
2. Find out about one kind of aircraft. Tell others in your section about it. It could be a commercial aircraft like Concorde or Airbus or a military aircraft like a Spitfire, Lynx or Chinook.
3. Talk to somebody who has flown in an aircraft, helicopter or hot air balloon. What was it like? If you have flown in an aircraft, tell others in your section about it.
4. Tell others in your section about an aircraft that you would like to fly in and why. It could be a real one or an aircraft you've thought up. You can use drawings or models to show others your aircraft.

Air Activities – stage 2
How to earn your badge
1. Learn the dangers you need to look out for when you're visiting an airfield.
2. Visit an airfield, air display or air museum.
3. Choose three of these to do:
   - Make and fly three different types of paper glider. Or you could make and fly a model aeroplane, hot air balloon or a kite.
   - Show you can spot six different airlines from their markings.
   - Point out and name the main parts of an aeroplane.
   - Point out and name different types of aircraft. They could be powered aeroplanes, airships, gliders or anything similar.
   - Fly in an aircraft. Tell the rest of your section about it.
   - Meet someone who flies regularly. Talk to them about their experiences.
   - Explain how different weather conditions can affect air activities.
   - Collect six pictures of different aircraft. Identify each aircraft from the pictures and share them with others in your section.

How to earn your badge

1. Learn the rules you have to follow when you're at an airfield. Draw a diagram or make a model of an airfield. Point out and name different points.

2. Learn the names of an aeroplane's control surfaces. Learn what these aircraft terms mean:
   - nose
   - fuselage
   - tail
   - wings
   - port
   - starboard
   - tailfin.

3. Build a chuck glider that can fly for at least five seconds. You can also build and fly a miniature hot air balloon or kite instead.

4. Choose one of these activities:
   - Collect photographs or pictures of six aircraft that interest you. Name them and explain what they're used for.
   - Talk about an airline that you are interested in or have travelled on. Show pictures of the airline's uniform and logos.

5. Take part in a visit to a place of aviation interest.

6. Talk to someone or spell your name using the phonetic alphabet. Why is the phonetic alphabet used in aviation?

7. Show how you would get a weather forecast for an air activity.
8. Using 1:50000 and 1:25000 Ordance Survey maps, show you understand the meaning of scale and common map symbols. Explain how a pilot might use a map differently from a car driver or somebody on a hike.

Air Activities – stage 4
How to earn your badge
1. Trim a paper aeroplane or model glider so it performs a straight glide, a stall and a turn.
2. Name the main control surfaces of an aeroplane. How do they work?
3. Point out six aircraft in use today. You can use pictures or spot them when they're in flight. At least two of the six must be civil commercial aircraft. One of the others must be a military aircraft. Another two must be light private aircraft.
4. Explain how wind speed and direction are measured. How does the weather affect air activities?
5. Explain the difference between a Mayday radio call and a Pan-Pan radio call. Give examples of when each might be used.
6. Show how to perform a pre-flight check on a light aircraft, microlight or glider. Explain why it's important to inspect each part.

7. Choose one of these activities:
   - Take part in a flight experience as a passenger. It could be in something like a light aircraft or a glider.
   - Help to organise a visit to an airfield or place of aviation history. It should be for a group of Beavers, Cubs, Scouts or Explorers. Explain what they will need to know before the visit.
8. Find out about the common types of charts used for flying. What are the conventional signs used on them?
9. Show how you do a take-off and landing using a home flight simulator computer programme with a joystick.
10. Draw a runway and its circuit patterns.

Air Activities – stage 5
How to earn your badge
1. Explain the relationship between lift, drag, thrust and weight.
2. Explain the duties of either:
   - an aircraft marshaller, demonstrating marshalling signals
   - a crew leader for a glider launch. Demonstrate their procedure and signals.
3. Imagine you're planning a cross-country flight of at least 60 nautical miles, at an air speed of 90 knots. What would the time of flight be from an overhead starting point to another overhead destination?

Your assessor will give you a head or tail wind to think about when you're working this out.

4. Choose one of these activities:
   - Explain the basic principles of a piston engine. Explain the four-stroke cycle, as well as valve and ignition timing.
   - Explain the differences between a piston engine and a jet engine. What's similar about them? Be sure to explain all the main parts and workings.

5. Explain how wind direction and strength is important in take-off and landing. Explain how a wing gives lift and why a wing stalls.

6. Build a scale model from a plastic kit, plans or photographs.

7. Take part in an air experience flight. Point out the landmarks that you fly over on an aviation chart.

8. Explain how temperature and atmospheric pressure are measured in weather forecasting.

9. Talk about basic cloud types. How they are they formed and why they're relevant to air activities.

How to earn your badge

1. Using plans, kits or by doing it from scratch, build and fly one of these:
   - rubber band powered model aircraft for 15 seconds
   - glider for 15 seconds
   - model airship
   - hovercraft
   - round the pole model (RTP).

2. Explain the emergency procedures for one type of aircraft. It could be something like a powered light aircraft, microlight, glider or small helicopter. What should you do in the event of engine failure, cable break or autorotation?

3. Find out why we need civilian airport security. What are main threats and the ways of dealing with them?

4. Explain how aircraft pressure instruments, altimeters and airspeed indicators work.

5. Explain how aircraft compasses and direction indicators work. What kind of errors can they give?

6. Identify the weather conditions associated with the movement of air masses over the UK. Find out about conditions like tropical, maritime and continental.

7. Interpret Met Office reports and forecasts for pilots. Find out about ways of reporting, like METAR and TAF.

8. Point out and name:
- signals used on a signals square
- runway and airfield markings
- light and pyrotechnics signals.

9. Find out why Morse code is still transmitted by navigational beacons. Learn to recognise six three-letter sequences.

10. Explain what trim is and why weight and balance is important.

11. Explain what flaps, slots and slats do and why they're on aircraft. Give examples of aircraft that use these devices.

12. Take an active part in at least three flying experiences, showing how you develop your skills with each flight.

COMMUNITY IMPACT

Making a difference is such an important part of being a Cub. The Community Impact staged activities give you the chance to help other people and make the world a better place.

Top tips

The Community Impact staged activities play a really important part in Scouting, so we've put together some special guidance for leaders so they can help and encourage you to complete the activities. You can find this on page 150.

The Community Impact Activities list online can help you decide on the best project for your community.

You can contact your councillor, Member of Parliament (UK), Assembly Member (Wales), Member of the Scottish Parliament (Scotland) or Member of the Legislative Assembly (Northern Ireland) using **theyworkforyou.com** or **writetothem.com**

You can find voluntary organisations who might support your community impact project on **stepuptoserve.org.uk**

Community Impact – stage 1

How to earn your badge

1. **Identify need**. Find out what issues and challenges exist in a community of your choice. You can help your local community, a community somewhere in the UK or a community in another country.

2. **Plan action**. Decide what issue your section should take action on. What do you want to change? What actions you would like to take? Talk to your section about it.

3. **Take action over three months**. You should:
   - spend at least four hours personally taking action on your chosen issue. It's better to spread your time out instead of doing it all in one go.
   - involve others in the action. Work in a team with your section and try to involve the people in the community you are trying to help.

4. **Learn and make more change**. Talk about what you've learned with your section. Talk about how you have made people's lives better. What could you do to help more people in the community?

5. **Tell the world.** Help other people to understand why the issue you took action on is important. Tell them what you did and how they can help.

How to earn your badge

1. **Identify need.** Find out what issues and challenges exist in a community of your choice. You can help your local community, a community somewhere in the UK or a community in another country.

2. **Plan action**. Decide what issue your section would like to take action on. What you would like to change? Involve a group of people who are not involved in Scouting and are passionate about your cause. Work together to plan action that will make things better.

3. **Take action over six months.** You should:
   - spend at least 12 hours personally taking action on your chosen issue. It's better to spread your time out instead of doing it all in one go.
   - involve others in the action. Work in a team with your section and people from the community you are trying to help.

4. **Learn and make more change.** Talk to your section about what you've learned and how you have made people's lives better. What could you do to help even more people in your chosen community?

5. **Tell the world.** Help other people to understand why the issue you have taken action on is important. Show what you did and how they can also help.

How to earn your badge

1. **Identify need.** Find out what issues and challenges exist in a community of your choice. You can help your local community, a community somewhere in the UK or a community in another country.

2. **Plan action.** Decide what issue your section would like to take action on. What you would like to change? Involve a group of people who are not involved in Scouting and are passionate about your cause. Work together to plan action that will make things better.

3. **Take action over nine months.** You should:
   - spend at least 24 hours in total personally taking action on your chosen issue. It's better to spread your time out instead of doing it all in one go.
   - involve others from your section and a group of non-Scouts, preferably from the community you are trying to help.

4. **Learn and make more change.** Talk about what you learned with your section. How have you made people's lives better? What could you do to help more people in your chosen community?

5. **Tell the world.** Help other people to understand why your chosen issue is important. Explain what you did and how they can also help.

How to earn your badge

1. **Identify need.** Find out what issues and challenges exist in a community of your choice. You can help your local community, a community somewhere in the UK or a community in another country.

2. **Plan action.** Decide what issue your section would like to take action on. What you would like to change? Involve a group of people who are not involved in Scouting and are passionate about your cause. Work together to plan action that will make things better.

3. **Take action over 12 months.** You should:
   - spend at least 48 hours personally taking action on your chosen issue. It's better to spread your time out over the year, instead of doing it all in one go.
   - involve your section and a group of non-Scouts, preferably people from the community you are trying to help.

4. **Learn and make more change.** Talk about what you learned with your section, how you have made people's lives better and what you could do to help more people in your chosen community.

5. **Tell the world.** Help other people to understand why your chosen issue is important. Explain how you have made a positive impact and how they can help.

DIGITAL CITIZEN

The digital world is part of our everyday lives. It helps us reach other people, learn new things and explore the world – all at the touch of a button or the swipe of a screen.

> There are rules and guidance around staying safe online that your leader will need to make sure you know. See page 153 to find out more.

Digital Citizen – stage 1

Complete every task to achieve Stage 1, showing that you have thought about the potential risks and how to stay safe for each activity.

How to earn your badge

1. Show that you can:
   - turn on and log into a computer
   - use a piece of software, for example email or a game
   - name the main parts of a computer system
   - connect a peripheral (for example a scanner or printer) to your computer and use it.
2. Create a piece of digital media. It could be artwork, a photograph, music or animation.

3. Use the internet for research:
   - decide on an area of interest.
   - find three websites with content that matches your area of interest.
   - collect information by printing or saving as files.
4. Using your internet research, design a presentation and tell others about what you have found out. This could be an electronic or paper based presentation

Digital Citizen – stage 2
How to earn your badge
Complete every task to achieve Stage 2, showing that you have thought about the potential risks and how to stay safe for each activity.

1. Plan and then create a piece of digital media. It could be music, animation, video, CAD (Computer Aided Design) or a 3D sculpture.
2. Show that you can:
   - send or reply to someone with a short email and include an attachment
   - download photos or other media from a camera or smart card
   - open and save a document then share it using a cloud service (like Google Docs or Microsoft Sharepoint) or a USB stick.

- create a document that includes media that you've downloaded or copied from another source.
3. Demonstrate how information online can be viewed and used by others once it has been posted/uploaded and how it is hard to remove.

Note: there is no requirement to post anything online yourself

Digital Citizen – stage 3
How to earn your badge
Complete every task to achieve Stage 3, showing that you have thought about the potential risks and how to stay safe for each activity.
1. Show that you know how to:
   - use anti-virus software
   - set up or adjust settings for accessibility and security
2. Use the internet for research:
   - decide on a specific area of interest
   - use at least two different search engines, using operators like AND, NOT and OR in the search box
   - collect information by using bookmarks
   - select specific, reliable information relevant to your area of research

- create a structured display of the information you have gathered. You could do this in a document, on a website or using a social tool such as Pinterest.
3. Plan, make, edit and share a piece of digital media based on your research. Share your research with other people, for example by email, on the web, by Multimedia Messaging Service or social media.
4. Create a multi-page website or social network group with your information. Present your information in a variety of ways. You could use infographics, images or graphs. You should then:
   - share your website with a wider audience
   - explain your sources of information and why you selected the details you chose
   - get some feedback on what you have done and make changes to improve your website based on that feedback.

Digital Citizen – stage 4
How to earn your badge
Complete every task to achieve Stage 4, showing that you have thought about the potential risks and how to stay safe for each activity.
1. Create a portfolio of digital media. It might include artwork or a photograph that you alter using creative tools, music, animation, CAD

(Computer Aided Design) or 3D sculpture.

2. Create a film, video, stop-motion animation or podcast and share it using a suitable media sharing tool.

3. Create a social network profile for your section, a band, local interest group or something similar. Alternatively you could make a small website that can host content, such as photos, poetry or information about your local area.

4. Use the internet for research:
   - choose a local, national, community or Scouting issue or something from the news or current affairs.
   - collect information from different sources, such as spreadsheets, databases, online news services and 'open access' data sources
   - put your information together in a structured way, for example grouping similar information. Make sure you know where each piece of information comes from.
   - select the information you think is most appropriate and reliable.

DIGITAL MAKER

Have you ever wondered how all those great apps, websites and games are made? Here's your chance to develop your own digital creations.

Some Digital Maker stages involve downloading stuff from the internet, which can be risky. Make sure you and your leader chat about the online safety rules on page 153.

Top tips
You can use any laptop, desktop computer, table or mobile device. It just needs to be able to perform what you need it to do. You could use different devices, operating systems or tools for different activities.

Digital Maker – stage 1
How to earn your badge
1. Show that you can identify a computer, the basic components inside a computer and what their purpose is.

2. Show that you can create instructions for something you do every day such as getting dressed in the morning or making a sandwich.

3. Design a game:
- use role play to act out how your digital game would work
- play the game with a group of friends and change the rules

4. Using paper, prototype a game and explain to someone how it works. Note: You could video your explanation

Digital Maker – stage 2
How to earn your badge

1. Design a robot to do a job done currently by a human. Perhaps a robot to put up a tent or tidy your bedroom.
- identify the sensors it will need, such as light, sound and movement sensors
- figure out what order the robot will need to complete tasks in

2. Show you understand that any data stored in a computer (such as text and images) are stored as binary. For example you could change a number into binary; create some pixel art or convert your name to binary.

3. Design an animation, game, app or electronic project. For example:
   - make a cartoon, animation or video of a game using a video camera or other equipment
   - design a sequence of a game, like a whole level or an in-game puzzle
   - design a level using craft materials or everyday objects and write out the rules (or pseudo code)
   - make a circuit using electronic components featuring at least one sensor, such as an automatic night light

Digital Maker – stage 3
How to earn your badge
1. Write a game or app for a programmable device. You should include:
   - event conditions (when your game reacts to something that happens)
   - iteration (when your code or instructions are repeated)
   - variables (for scoring, health or counting things within the game).
   - discuss your development and how you overcame any bugs. Useful sources include: Micobit (**microbit.co.uk/**) Codebug (**codebug.org.uk/**) or Raspberry Pi- (**raspberrypi.org/**)

2. Show you understand that sound and video can be stored as data. You could do this by recording and editing sound and/or video.
3. Design and build:
   - a digital device with a purpose or
   - a robot using pre built components. (such as the mBot - learn.makeblock.com/en/mbot/)

Digital Maker – stage 4
How to earn your badge
1. Set up a home network and connect it to the internet.
2. Install or run an alternative operating system on a computer. Alternatively, use a 'Live DVD' or a USB stick.
3. Design a game:
   - build a game that includes progression and is fun and interesting to play
   - get someone else to play and evaluate it
4. Make a robot using a kit with components that respond to sensor input (for example, a robot that backs away from an object in it's path)
5. Create a prototype for an App and identify:
   - the functions it would perform
   - who the users would be
   - the purpose
   - the variables

How to earn your badge

1. Install the software to run a web server and host a webpage on a computer or other device. Tools like LAMP, WAMP or Google's Webserver project for the Raspberry Pi could help you. You can find these for free online.

2. Make a game or app that serves a purpose. It should:
   - have a clear objective
   - be challenging for the user
   - have a clear sense of progression
   - keep a score
   - offer a reward to the user for playing (for example the score could unlock levels or icons).

   For an App it should:
   - have a clear objective
   - be created for social good
   - have a clear user journey

3. Make your own bespoke robot that responds to the environment. For example, a robot that reacts to light, sight or its proximity to other objects.

EMERGENCY AID

When accidents cause someone
to get hurt, it can make a huge
difference if you know what to do.

Learn how to help care for others and yourself in
an emergency.

Emergency Aid – stage 1
How to earn your badge
Show you understand all of the actions listed.

Explain to you leader or another adult about:
- the importance of getting help
- what to say when you call 999
- helping someone who is unconscious
- helping someone who is bleeding
- reassuring someone at the scene of
  an emergency.

Emergency Aid – stage 2
How to earn your badge
Show you understand all of the actions listed.

1. Explain to your leader or another adult about:
   - the importance of getting help
   - what to say when you call 999
   - reassuring someone at the scene of
     an emergency.

2. Explain how to help someone who:
   - is unconscious
   - is bleeding
   - has a burn
   - is having an asthma attack.

If you hold a first aid award covering this or a similar syllabus from a recognised first aid provider (such as the British Red Cross or St John Ambulance) you can automatically get this badge.

Emergency Aid – stage 3
How to earn your badge
You will need to take part in around two to three hours of training, which should be taught by a trained adult.

1. Explain to your leader or another adult about how to call 999.
2. Explain how you help someone who:
   - is unconscious
   - is unconscious and not breathing
   - is bleeding
   - has a burn
   - has heat exhaustion
   - has hypothermia
   - is choking
   - is having an asthma attack.

If you hold a first aid award covering this or a similar syllabus from a recognised first aid provider (such as the British Red Cross or St John Ambulance) you can automatically get this badge.

Emergency Aid – stage 4
How to earn your badge
You will need to take part in around three to six hours of training, which should be taught by a trained adult.

1. Explain to your Leader or another adult about how to call 999.
2. Explain how you help someone who:
   - is unconscious
   - is unconscious and not breathing
   - is bleeding
   - has a burn
   - has heat exhaustion
   - has hypothermia
   - is choking
   - is having an asthma attack
   - is having a heart attack
   - has a head injury
   - has a suspected spinal injury
   - has a broken bone
   - has a sprain or strain
   - has meningitis.

If you hold a first aid award covering this or a similar syllabus from a recognised first aid provider (such as the British Red Cross or St John Ambulance) you can automatically get this badge.

You must take part in formal training to gain this badge - a first aid award covering this or a similar syllabus. Your training must be from a recognised first aid provider, such as the British Red Cross or St Johns Ambulance, or someone qualified to deliver First Response.

Emergency Aid – stage 5
How to earn your badge

You will need to take part in around six to eight hours of training, which should be taught by a trained adult.

1. Explain to your leader or another adult about how to call 999.
2. Explain how you help someone who:
   - is unconscious
   - is unconscious and not breathing
   - is bleeding
   - has a burn
   - has heat exhaustion
   - has hypothermia
   - is choking
   - is having an asthma attack

- is having a heart attack
- has a head injury
- has a suspected spinal injury
- has a broken bone
- has a sprain or strain
- has meningitis
- is having a stroke
- is experiencing a diabetic emergency
- is having a severe allergic reaction
- is having a seizure.

If you hold a first aid award covering this or a similar syllabus from a recognised first aid provider (such as the British Red Cross or St John Ambulance) you can automatically get this badge.

You must take part in formal training to gain this badge - a first aid award covering this or a similar syllabus. Your training must be from a recognised first aid provider, such as the British Red Cross or St Johns Ambulance.

HIKES AWAY

Your first hike away is an amazing milestone, which deserves to be recognised. And as you do more hikes away, you can pick up other badges.

How to earn your badge
There are eight different badges you can collect. Each one marks a certain number of hikes or journeys you will have completed:

1   2   5   10   15   20   35   50

Each hike or journey must involve at least three hours of activity and have a purpose, which you will agree with your Leader. The sorts of activity that count as a hike away include:
- following a towpath trail and discovering how locks work on a local canal
- exploring a local town or village while you're on camp or a Pack holiday
- walking up a hill and enjoying the view.

! You must be properly dressed and equipped for the weather conditions and terrain. Your leader will also need to make sure you're following the rules in chapter nine of the Policy and Organisation Rules and the Activity Permit Scheme.

MUSICIAN

A piano playing maestro, a guitar hero or singing sensation – whatever you want to be, practice and perform as a musician with these great activities.

Musician – stage 1

How to earn your badge

1. Skill.
- Listen to a short tune of a couple of lines and then sing it back.
- Listen to another tune and then beat or clap out the rhythm.

2. Performance. Sing or play two different types of song or tune on your chosen instrument – remember your voice is an instrument too. You must perform in front of other people. They could be from Scouting or the audience at a group show or school concert.

West Favou 8/6/18 — *Happy Birthday Twinkle Twinkle*

3. Knowledge.
- Demonstrate some of the musical exercises that you use to practice your skills.
- Talk about your instrument and why you enjoy playing it. If you sing, talk about the songs you sing and why you enjoy them.

4. Interest. Tell your assessor about the music that you most like to listen to.

How to earn your badge

1. **Skill.** Reach Grade One standard for the Associated Board of the Royal School of Music (or similar). It can be on an instrument of your choice or by singing.

2. **Performance.** Sing or play two different types of song or tune on your chosen instrument. You must perform in front of other people either in Scouting or at a public performance such as at a group show or school concert.

3. **Knowledge.**
   - Demonstrate some of the musical exercises that you use to practice your skills.
   - Talk about your instrument and why you enjoy playing it. If you sing, talk about the songs you sing and why you enjoy them.
   - Name a piece of music associated with your instrument.
   - Name several musicians who you have heard.

4. **Interest.** Talk about your own interests in music. Share what you listen to most and how it's similar or different to the music you play or sing.

Musician – stage 3

How to earn your badge

1. **Skill.** Reach Grade Two standard for the Associated Board of the Royal School of Music (or similar). It can be on an instrument of your choice or by singing.

2. **Performance.** Sing or play, as a solo or with others, two different types of tune on your chosen instrument. You must perform in front of other people. They could be from Scouting or an audience at a group show or school concert.

3. **Knowledge.**
   - Demonstrate some of the musical exercises that you use to practice your skills.
   - Talk about your instrument and why you enjoy playing it. If you sing, talk about the songs you sing and why you enjoy singing them.
   - Talk about three well-known pieces of music associated with your instrument or chosen songs.

4. **Interest.** Talk about your own interests in music. Share what you listen to most. How is it similar to or different from the music you play or sing?

Musician – stage 4
How to earn your badge
1. **Skill.** Reach Grade Three standard for the Associated Board of the Royal School of Music (or similar). It can be on an instrument of your choice or by singing.
2. **Performance.** Sing or play three different types of song or tune on your chosen instrument. One should be a solo and one should be played with other musicians in an arrangement of your choice. Your performance should be public. It could be a group show or school concert.
3. **Knowledge.**
   - Demonstrate some of the musical exercises that you use to practice your skills.
   - Talk about your instrument and why you enjoy playing it. If you sing, talk about the songs you sing and why you enjoy them.
   - Talk about some of the musicians who are associated with your instrument.
4. **Interest.** Talk about your own interests in music. Share what you listen to most. How is it similar to or different from the music you play or sing?

Musician – stage 5
How to earn your badge

1. **Skill.** Reach Grade Five standard for the Associated Board of the Royal School of Music (or similar) on the instrument of your choice or by singing.

2. **Performance.** Sing or play three different types of song or tune on your chosen instrument. One should be a solo and one should be played with other musicians in an arrangement of your choice. Your performance should be public. It could be a group show or school concert.

3. **Knowledge.**
   - Demonstrate some of the musical exercises that you use to practise your skills.
   - Talk about your instrument and why you enjoy playing it. Alternatively, talk about the songs you sing and why you enjoy singing them.
   - Name several well-known pieces of music associated with your instrument.
   - Name several musicians associated with your instrument.

4. **Interest.** Talk about your own interests in music. Share what you listen to most. How is it similar to or different from the music you play or sing?

NAUTICAL SKILLS

Aye-aye captain… Set sail or row
your boat out on the open water.

Nautical Skills – stage 1
How to earn your badge
1. Take part in a water activity taster session.
   You could try:
   - paddle sports
   - rafting
   - sailing
   - windsurfing
   - pulling.
2. Point out and name the different equipment
   used for the activity you chose.
3. Learn about the safety equipment used.

Nautical Skills – stage 2
How to earn your badge
1. Take part in a water activity taster session for
   at least one hour. By the end of the session you
   should be comfortable in your craft.
   You could try:
   - paddle sports
   - rafting
   - sailing
   - windsurfing
   - pulling.

2. Show that you understand what to do if a capsize or man overboard happens in your chosen activity.
3. Demonstrate that you can tie either a figure of eight or a reef knot. Describe how you use them in water activities.
4. Name the basic equipment you used during your chosen activity.
5. List some clothing that is not suitable for your chosen activity, and explain the reasons why.
6. Show that you know the safety equipment you used and why it's needed.

Nautical Skills – stage 3
How to earn your badge
1. Take part in at least two one-hour taster sessions in two different water based activities. By the end of the session you should be competent at controlling your craft. You could try:
   - canoeing
   - a powered activity like yachting
   - pulling
   - sailing
   - windsurfing.
2. Show that you know how to act safely in your chosen activity if you are involved in a capsize or man overboard situation.
3. Show how to check the depth of the water so that you don't ground or beach. Try a method normally used in your activity.

4. Show how to tie a clove hitch, a bowline knot, and a round turn and two half-hitches. Explain when these would be used.
5. Name the parts of one type of watercraft.
6. What clothing should you wear for your chosen activity? Talk about them and demonstrate what you should wear.
7. Explain the basic safety rules for your chosen activity.
8. Explain the difference between a buoyancy aid and a life jacket. When should each of them be used and how do they function? Show how they are worn.

Nautical Skills – stage 4
How to earn your badge
1. Develop your skills in two water-based activities. Show competency and technique in:
   - launching and recovering a watercraft
   - manoeuvring a watercraft
   - communicating with the group
   - knowledge of safety.
2. Take part in a capsize and recovery drill for the two watercraft you have chosen.
3. Use a throw bag or line to reach a person six metres away in the water.
4. Show you know how to apply the steering rules to your chosen watercraft. Show you recognise the main channel markers.

5. Use a knot or a cleat correctly to moor a boat with a painter or mooring line. If you tie a knot, it must be either a round turn and two half hitches or a bowline. Describe what you need to be aware of when using these to moor.

6. Complete one of these:
- Pipe the 'still' and 'carry on' on a Bosun's call.
- Make a sail maker's whipping and one other type of whipping. Safely heat-seal the end of a rope. Describe the correct use of these whippings.
- Make an eye splice or a back splice. Safely heat-seal the end of a rope. Describe the correct use of these splices.

7. Name the parts of your chosen watercraft. If you have completed Nautical Skills Stage 3 you must choose a different watercraft.

8. Take part in a challenging three-hour expedition or exercise afloat.

9. Take part in a competition or crew-based activity in your chosen watercraft.

Nautical Skills – stage 5
How to earn your badge

1. Develop your skills in one water-based activity to a level where you can operate the watercraft safely. You could gain a personal permit or a national governing body personal competency award to show you have these skills.

2. Take part in a simple rescue exercise to show how you would use your watercraft to recover others from the water.

3. Show that you know about pilotage, navigation lights, sound signals, tides, currents and eddies, depending on what's relevant to your local waterways.

4. Show that you can tie a figure-of-eight knot, clove hitch, and a round turn and two half hitches. Show that you can tie another three knots: sheet bend, rolling hitch and bowline, then describe their uses.

5. Explain the different types of ropes used in water activities, their advantages and disadvantages and how to care for them.

6. Do one of these activities:
   - Make a rope fender or other piece of decorative rope work, such as a lanyard or a decorative knot.
   - Demonstrate three calls made on a Bosun's pipe, other than 'still' and 'carry on'.
   - Hoist the colours for a Sea Scout ceremonial or nautical themed ceremony.

7. Plan and take part in a one-day expedition or exercise afloat with others.

8. Learn how different boats communicate with each other where you are.

9. Take on the helm or cox role in a watercraft or help prepare a team for a competition.

10. Learn how to get local weather forecasts. Find out why they're important and learn to recognise signs of changing weather.
11. Learn how to stay safe against the effects of cold, and how to recognise and treat hypothermia.

Nautical Skills – stage 6
How to earn your badge

1. Develop your skills in one water-based activity to a level where you can operate the watercraft safely. You could demonstrate this by gaining a personal permit. If you have completed Nautical Skills Stage 5, you should try a different water based activity.
2. Learn about flares, distress signals and marine VHF radio. When is it appropriate to use them?
3. Learn about and explain the access and mooring issues in your chosen activity.
4. Learn about and explain the 'nautical rules of the road' including passing other watercraft, the International Rules for Preventing Collisions at Sea (IRPCS), light signals, sound signals and the use of channels.
5. Show that you know how to maintain your watercraft. Show you can carry out simple repairs over the course of three months.
6. Plan and take part in an overnight expedition with others by water. Your time underway should be at least six hours.

NAVIGATOR

Lead your team, take charge and
set the course for an adventure.
With your keen sense of direction
and your Navigator staged activity
badge, you need never lose your way.

How to earn your badge
1. Find where you are on a simple map. You could
   use a map of a local park, nature reserve, zoo or
   even a theme park.
2. Point out a number of features or locations on
   that map. You could pinpoint places like the
   toilets, car park, bird hide or picnic area.
3. Learn the four cardinal points of a compass.
4. Draw a simple map of where you live, your
   meeting place or another area local to you.
5. Use a map during an outdoor activity.
6. Show you understand what you need to wear
   for the activity, and what equipment you and
   the adults will need.

1. Learn how to read a four-figure grid reference.
2. Understand how to use the key of a map.
3. Use a map during an outdoor activity.

4. Draw a simple map to direct someone from your meeting place to a local point of interest.
5. With other Cubs, go for a walk with a leader around the local area. Take it in turns to use one of these methods of navigation:
   - written instructions
   - recorded instructions
   - road signs
   - tracking signs
   - maps.
6. Learn the eight points of a compass. Use them in an activity.
7. Show you know what clothes to wear for the activities involved in this badge. What equipment you and the adults need on the activities?

Navigator – stage 3
How to earn your badge
1. Learn how to read a six-figure grid reference.
2. Understand contour lines on an Ordnance Survey map.
3. Using 1:50000 and 1:25000 scale Ordnance Survey maps, show that you understand the meaning of scale. Show that you can set the map to north and recognise conventional map symbols.
4. Follow and walk a route of at least 5 kilometres, using a map to navigate for at least part of the journey.

Your leader can plan the route but you'll work with other Cubs, or take turns, to navigate.

5. Show you know what to wear for the walk. Explain what kit you and your group will need.

How to earn your badge

1. Show you know how to:
   - convert grid bearings to magnetic bearings. Do the same thing the other way round.
   - use back bearings to check the route.
   - estimate your current position using a compass
   - walk on a bearing. Show you can also 'deviate from course' by using the four right angles technique to get round an obstacle.
   - read a six-figure grid reference.

2. Using 1:50000 and 1:25000 scale Ordnance Survey maps:
   - look at contour lines to find out what the shape and steepness is of the land. Learn what the topographical features mean, including valley, col, ridge and spur.
   - show how to set a map, with and without a compass. Learn how to use and give six-figure grid references. Show how you would use a roamer to improve accuracy.
   - show how to find north without a compass, by day or night.

3. Walk two compass routes of at least 5 kilometres each. They should both be defined on a map. You can define one route's start and end points. An adult can define the other route.
4. Show you know how what to wear for the walk. What kit you and your group need?
5. Choose the best kind of map for the journey you are taking.

Navigator – stage 5
How to earn your badge

1. Using a 1:25000 scale Ordnance Survey map and compass, navigate along a course of at least six 'legs' to the standard of the Hill and Moorland Leader Award. You're not expected to hold this award – just have a look at the course to get an idea of the level you need to achieve. Find out more at mountain-training.org
2. Using only a compass and pacing, successfully navigate a course of at least four 'legs'.
3. Using only a map, successfully navigate a course of at least four 'legs'.
4. Make two sketch maps. One should be of a city or town and one of countryside or a country village. They should both help a stranger to travel from one place to another.
5. Finish at least three different orienteering courses in a reasonable time.

6. Complete a full route plan for a 20km hill-walking route. The route should be set by an adult with the right knowledge. It should take place in terrain one or terrain two, details of which can be found in Policy Organisation and Rules.

7. Show that you know what clothing and equipment you need for your journey.

NIGHTS AWAY

Setting off on an overnight expedition gives you a real feeling of freedom. These staged badges recognise the nights away you have been on.

How to earn your badges
You can pick up a badge each time you reach these numbers of nights away:

1	2	3	4	5	10
15	20	35	50	75	100
125	150	175	200		

These are for recognised Cub activities, sleeping in tents, bivouacs, hostels, on boats or at other centres.

! You must have the proper equipment for your activity and the weather.

PADDLE SPORTS

Paddle sports are a fantastic, fun way to explore rivers, canals and lakes. You can build on your skills in either a canoe or a kayak, working with other people if you need to..

Paddle Sports – stage 1
How to earn your badge
1. Name different types of paddle craft.
2. Name three places you could safely go canoeing or kayaking.
3. Take part in a warm up activity to prepare you for canoeing or kayaking. You could practise balancing whilst kneeling. You could also get in and out of a boat or practise a paddling action.
4. Dress properly for your chosen activity. Show you know why buoyancy aids are important. Show how to put one on correctly.
5. Take part in a taster session that covers:
   • naming equipment used and the parts of the boat
   • getting into and out of a boat safely
   • balancing a boat
   • manoeuvring your boat in different directions, including moving forward

If you have done the British Canoeing's Paddle Power Start you can get this badge without doing the steps.

You can do most of these steps without actually being on the water. But we think it's best to do them as part of a practical paddle sports activity.

Your leader will find lots of activities in Programmes Online as well as on the BCU website.
Visit **http://tiny.cc/lqzzmx**

Paddle Sports – stage 2
How to earn your badge
Before you attempt Stage 2, you need to have completed all the steps for Paddle Sports Stage 1.

You can then earn your Paddle Sports Stage 2 badge by doing these six tasks.
1. Lift, carry and launch a boat.
2. Paddle forward in a straight line.
3. Show you can steer around a course.
4. Show you can stop the boat safely.
5. Show you can exit the boat onto the shore safely.
6. Capsize, swim to the shore and empty the boat of water.

If you have done the British Canoeing's Paddle Power Passport you can get this badge without doing the steps.

How to earn your badge
Before you attempt Stage 3, you need to have completed all the steps for Paddle Sports Stage 2.

You can then earn your Paddle Sports Stage 3 badge by doing these eight tasks.

1. With help, show more than one safe method for lifting and carrying your boat.
2. Demonstrate two different ways of safely launching your boat.
3. Show you can get in and out of your boat without help.
4. Paddle forwards and backwards in a straight line, keeping good posture.
5. Show you can steer around a figure of eight course.
6. Show you can stop the boat safely when it's moving back and forth.
7. Capsize, swim to the shore and empty the boat of water.
8. Assist someone else back into their boat following a capsize.

If you have done the British Canoeing's Paddle Power Discover you can get Stage 3 and Stage 4 of this badge without doing the steps.

How to earn your badge

Before you attempt Stage 4, you need to have completed all the steps for Paddle Sports Stage 3.

You can then earn your Paddle Sports Stage 4 badge by doing these two tasks.

1. Choose two of the disciplines below. Paddle your boat for at least 200 metres for both of your chosen disciplines:
   • crew. Choose from K2 (two man kayak), K4 (four man kayak), C2 (two man canoe) or OC2 (two man canoe with outrigger).
   • flat water
   • white water
   • touring
   • short boat
   • ergo.

2. Take part in at least two activities from the list. They should both be something you haven't tried before:
   • freestyle
   • marathon
   • polo
   • slalom
   • sprint
   • surf
   • time trial
   • wild water.

SAILING

Build up the skills to explore the seas as you work your way through these staged sailing badges.

Sailing – stage 1
How to earn your badge

1. Name some different types of sailing crafts.
2. Name three places you could safely go sailing.
3. Take part in a warm up activity to prepare you for a sailing activity. You could try tacking and gybing or hiking out. You could also try a syncro-jump to cross the boat together in a tack or gybe.
4. Dress properly for a sailing activity. Show that you know why buoyancy aids are important. Show how to put one on correctly.
5. Take part in a taster session. By the end you should be able to:
   • name equipment used and parts of the boat
   • get into and out of a boat safely
   • balance a boat
   • manoeuvre your boat in different directions, including moving forward.

You can complete most of these steps without actually being on the water, although it's best to complete them as part of a sailing activity.

If you have done the RYA Youth Sailing Scheme Stage 1 you can get this badge without doing the steps.

Sailing – stage 2
How to earn your badge
Before you attempt Stage 2, you need to have completed all the steps for Sailing Stage 1.

You can then earn your Sailing Stage 2 badge by doing these five tasks.

1. Launch and recover your dinghy.
2. Control the direction and speed of your dinghy to steer around a course.
3. Stop your dinghy safely.
4. Capsize and get to the shore safely. Recover the dinghy.
5. Show you can moor your dinghy.

If you have done the RYA Youth Sailing Scheme Stage 2 you can get this badge without doing the steps.

How to earn your badge

Before you attempt Stage 3, you need to have completed all the steps for Sailing Stage 2.

You can then earn your Sailing Stage 3 badge by doing these seven tasks. Try to use a different boat to the one you used for Stage 2.

If you're using a keelboat, you don't have to do steps 1-3.

1. Prepare, launch and recover your boat in an onshore wind.
2. Show the correct way to store your boat ashore.
3. Show you can right a capsized dinghy as helm or crew.
4. Show you know how to recover a man overboard.
5. Show that you're able to do these tasks:
   - sail setting
   - balance
   - trim
   - course made good
   - centreboard
   - aking upwind
   - gybing from a training run
   - coming alongside a moored boat
   - picking up a mooring.

6. Learn how a sail works and its basic aerodynamics.

7. Show that you can know the meaning of words used when sailing, such as windward, leeward and bear away.

You can get this badge without doing the steps if you hold The Scout Association Personal Activity Permit for Dinghy Sailing or the RYA Youth Sailing Scheme Stage 3.

Sailing – stage 4
How to earn your badge
1. Launch and recover your boat in any wind direction.

2. Set up your boat according to weather conditions, using sail and rig controls.

3. Show that you're able to recover a man overboard.

4. Show that you know about:
- International Regulations for Preventing Collision at Sea (IRPCS)
- Beaufort Scale
- synoptic charts
- tidal ebb and flow
- spring and neap tides.

If you have done the RYA Youth Sailing Scheme Stage 4 you can get this badge without doing the steps.

SWIMMER

Is it a seal? Is it a dolphin? No, it's you! You can swim through the water with speed and skill, with plenty of practice and a little confidence.

Swimmer – stage 1
How to earn your badge

1. Learn the general safety rules for swimming, such as not diving into shallow water or not swimming on your own. Find out where is safe to swim locally.
2. Show you know how to prepare for swimming, such as taking part in a warm up.
3. Show how to make a controlled entry into the water without using the steps. The water must be at least 1.5 metres deep.
4. Swim 10 metres on your front.
5. Tread water for 30 seconds in an upright position.
6. Use a buoyancy aid to float still in the water for 30 seconds.
7. Show that you're able to retrieve an object from chest-deep water.
8. Perform a push and glide on both your front and back.
9. Swim 25 metres without stopping.
10. Take part in an organised swimming activity.

✓ Signed dl
9/6/18

Swimmer – stage 2
How to earn your badge

1. Learn the general safety rules for swimming, such as not diving into shallow water or not swimming on your own. Find out where is safe to swim locally.
2. Show you know how to prepare for swimming, such as taking part in a warm up.
3. Show how to make a controlled entry or dive from the side of the pool. It must be into at least 1.5 metres of water.
4. Swim 10 metres on your front and 10 metres on your back. Then swim 10 metres on your back using only your legs.
5. Tread water for three minutes in an upright position.
6. Surface dive into at least 1.5 metres of water. Touch the bottom of the pool with both hands.
7. Mushroom float for ten seconds.
8. Enter the pool and push off from the side on your front. Glide for five metres.
9. From the side of the pool, push off on your back and glide for as far as possible.
10. Swim 100 metres without stopping.
11. Take part in an organised swimming activity.

Swimmer – stage 3
How to earn your badge

1. Learn the general safety rules for swimming, such as not diving into shallow water or not swimming on your own. Find out where is safe to swim locally.
2. Show you know how to prepare for exercises. You could do this by leading a warm up.
3. Show how to do a controlled entry or dive from the side of the pool. It must be into at least 1.5 metres of water.
4. Swim for 50 metres in shirt and shorts.
5. Tread water for three minutes with one hand behind your back.
6. Surface dive into 1.5 metres of water. Recover an object with both hands from the bottom. Return to the side of the pool, holding the object in both hands.
7. Enter the water from the side of the pool by sliding in from a sitting position. Take up and hold the heat escape lessening posture for five minutes. You can use any floating object for support.
8. Swim 400 metres without stopping.
9. Take part in a different organised swimming activity to the one on your previous swimming badge.

Swimmer – stage 4

How to earn your badge

1. Learn the general safety rules for swimming, such as not diving into shallow water or not swimming on your own. Find out where is safe to swim locally.

2. Show you know how to prepare for exercises. You could do this by leading a warm up.

3. Show how to do a racing dive into at least 1.8 metres of water. Then straddle jump into at least 2 meters of water.

4. Swim 100 metres in less than four minutes.

5. Tread water for five minutes.

6. Surface dive into 1.5 metres of water, head first and then feet first. Swim at least 5 metres underwater on both occasions.

7. Enter the water in the way you would if you didn't know the depth. Swim 10 metres to a floating object. Use the object to take up and hold the heat escape lessening posture for five minutes.

8. Swim 800 metres using any of the four recognised strokes without stopping. You should swim 400m on your front and 400m on your back.

9. Take part in an organised swimming activity. It should be different to any activities for previous swimming badges.

How to earn your badge

1. Learn the general safety rules for swimming, such as not diving into shallow water or not swimming on your own. Find out where is safe to swim locally.

2. Show you know how to prepare for exercises. You could do this by leading a warm up.

3. Show how to do a racing dive into at least 1.8 metres of water. Then do a straddle jump into at least 2 meters of water.

4. Swim 100 metres in shirt and shorts. When you've finished, take off the shirt and shorts and climb out of the pool without help. Your time limit is three minutes.

5. Tread water for five minutes. For three of the minutes you must hold one arm clear of the water.

6. Scull on your back, head first, for 10 metres. Do the same again, feet first, for 10 metres. Move into a tuck position and turn 360 degrees, keeping your head out of the water.

7. Swim 10 metres, then perform a somersault without touching the side of the pool. Carry on swimming in the same direction for a further 10 metres.

8. Show how to do the heat escape lessening posture.

9. Show how to do a surface dive, both head and feet first, into 1.5 metres of water.

10. Swim 1,000 metres using any of the four recognised strokes, for a minimum distance of 200 metres per stroke. This swim must be completed in 35 minutes.
11. Take part in an organised swimming activity. It must be a different activity to any one you've taken part in for a previous swimming badge.

TIME ON THE WATER

If you're building up your experience in boating or water sport activities, you can gain badges to recognise your achievement as you go.

How to earn your badges

You can collect Time on the Water staged badges when you take part in any of these activities, as long as each session lasts about 1-2 hours:

- kayaking
- canoeing
- sailing
- windsurfing
- powerboating
- kiteboarding
- surfing
- yachting
- motorcruising

- narrowboating
- pulling or rowing
- paddleboarding
- white water rafting
- traditional rafting.

And as you complete the following number of activities, you can gain a badge:

1	2	5	10
15	20	35	50

! You must be properly dressed and equipped for your activity and the weather conditions. Your leader will also need to make sure you're following the activity rules in chapter nine of the Policy and Organisation Rules and the Activity Permit Scheme.

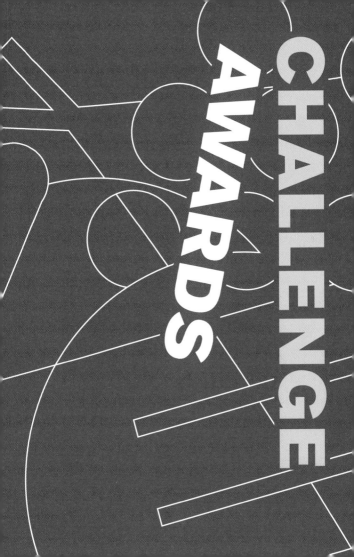

CHALLENGE AWARDS

BE THE BEST YOU CAN BE...

Awards
Badges aren't the only way you can be rewarded in Cubs. You can earn awards as you go through Cubs and take part in special challenges. They all help to make your time in Cubs fun, interesting and worthwhile.

And as you earn them, you can work towards the big one – the Chief Scout's Silver Award.

Challenge Awards
There are seven awards in the Cub section. They're different to the other badges because you'll do these with other Cubs, rather than outside of meetings or at home.

OUR ADVENTURE CHALLENGE AWARD

How to earn your award

1. Take part in two different
adventurous activities. At least
one of them should be new to
you. You could try:

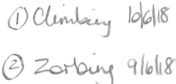

- crate stacking
- caving
- abseiling
- grass sledging
- bouldering
- rafting
- bell boating
- fencing
- zorbing.

① Climbing 10/6/18

② Zorbing 9/6/18

2. Take part in six other outdoor activities.
At least two of them should be new to you.
You could try:

- flying a kite you have made
- making and lighting a fire
- following a sensory trail
- making a hot air balloon and flying it
- making a ballista
- playing some water games
- going on an obstacle course
- tracking
- making a mini raft.

① ✓
② ✓
③ ✓
4/5/8 ④ cycling
5/6/18 ⑤ skatepark
3/6/18 ⑥ Bead race 1 mile

3. Go on a hike or follow a trail. Try to walk for about 1-2 hours.
4. Prepare for your activities and hikes. Find out what you need to wear and bring, and pack your own bag. You will need to know what you have with you, and remember everything you need.

Top tips
If you enjoyed this challenge award, why not try these activity badges?
- Cyclist
- Equestrian
- Skater
- Water Activities

You could do your adventurous activities as part of a District or County fun day, on a camp, a residential opportunity or as part of a Pack meeting.

Adventurous activities don't have to be expensive to be exciting. Just try something new.

Add some fun to your walk or hike by using maps and compasses to explore the area.

OUR OUTDOORS CHALLENGE AWARD

How to earn your award

1. Take an active part in at least three nights away, on camps or Pack holidays.
2. While you're away, work with other Cubs to do all of these tasks:
   - help to pitch and strike your tent
   - show that you know how to look after yourself and be safe at camp
   - show that you know how to keep your tent and kit safe, tidy and secure
   - cook a meal with your Six
   - build a shelter big enough for two Cubs
   - using bamboos canes, rubber bands or simple lashings complete a simple pioneering project or make a camp gadget
   - learn and follow the Countryside Code
   - show you know what things you need to do to look after your campsite, and that you can put them into practise
   - show that you know how to treat mild burns, scalds, cuts or grazes and make a call to the emergency services.

3. While you're away, do at least two of these tasks
   as well:
   - take part in a wide game
   - take part in a campfire sing-along or other
     entertainment
   - cook a backwoods meal
   - build a bivouac and sleep in it
   - care for your personal equipment while
     at camp
   - using knots that you've learned, make a
     simple camp gadget, like a flagpole.

Top tips

If you enjoyed this challenge award, why not try
these activity badges?
   - Backwoods Cooking
   - Pioneer

A camp or pack holiday gives you the chance to
do things you wouldn't be able to do on a normal
meeting night. You could go away with your own
Pack, another Pack or as part of a Group, District or
County event.

If you can't stay away overnight for any reason,
talk to your leader. They might be able to arrange
another way you can take part and do the tasks.

OUR SKILLS CHALLENGE AWARD

How to earn your award

1. Try two new sports or physical activities at least once.
   You could try:
   - tennis
   - dance
   - basketball
   - tai chi.
2. Take part in three activities to help you be healthy, like:
   - healthy eating
   - exercise
   - learning how the human body works ③ *Race for Life 12/6/18*
   - another activity agreed with your leader.
3. Pick two creative things to try, and show your leader what you've done. You could:
   - write a short story ①
   - make a model ② *model tree 11/6/18*
   - take some photos and use them to tell a story
   - be part of a play or sketch.
4. Learn and use at least four of these skills:
   - sew on a button or badge
   - make cakes, bread, biscuits or something similar ①
   - oil a bicycle chain, change a wheel or fit lights
   - make a cup of tea or coffee, then wash up afterwards

10/6/18

- lay a table for a meal
- peel potatoes or other vegetables
- iron your scarf
- change a lightbulb, in a table or standard lamp
- clean a window
- tidy and clean your bedroom
- another similar home skill agreed with your leader.

5. Take part in at least two problem solving activities that you haven't done before. It should be something that you need to think creatively for. As part of the activity you need to say what you found difficult, what you did to solve the problem, and why.

Top tips

If you enjoyed this challenge award, why not try these activity badges?

- Artist
- Athletics
- Athletics Plus
- Book Reader
- Chef
- Collector
- DIY
- Entertainer
- Hobbies
- Home Help
- Martial Arts
- Photographer

- Physical Recreation
- Scientist
- Sports Enthusiast

Your home skills for number 4 could be done on a normal meeting night or on camp, or you could do them at home and bring in pictures.

For number 5, you could build a small bridge across a stream, make an egg timer out of unusual materials, design and make a model with at least two moving parts, make a model raft that can float with a lit candle on it, or make and solve a code.

OUR WORLD
CHALLENGE AWARD

How to earn your award

1. Make a list of the services for people in your local area. Find out a bit about them, and visit one if possible.
2. Work with people or an organisation from a community. Take the chance to find an issue that your Pack could help with. It should be something that helps people and also helps you grow as a person. Plan and carry out the project with your Pack and others in the community. Then share what you learned from the activity with other people.

Talk about how it helped other people and what you will do with the skills and experiences you have gained.

3. Take part in an act of worship, reflection or celebration.

4. Find out about a faith or culture other than your own. You could visit places of worship or ceremony.

5. Talk about a time when you did your best. Explain how you have kept your Cub Promise and the Law.

6. Take part in an activity about the environment.

7. Try a game played by Cubs in a different country, and learn their Promise.

8. Celebrate a festival from another country. You might make (and eat!) some special food, make something relating to the festival or visit somewhere special.

Top tips
If you enjoyed this challenge award, why not try these activity badges?
- Animal Carer
- Astronomer
- Communicator
- Disability Awareness
- Environmental Conservation
- Fire Safety
- Home Safety
- International

- Local Knowledge
- My Faith
- Naturalist
- Personal Safety
- Road Safety
- World Faiths
- World Issues

There are lots of fun ways to create a list for number 1. You could use pictures, drama, go for a walk around town, make a map and mark out the services or play a game.

For number 2, you could pick up litter in your local park, raise money to help a local hospital or take part in a local community event. Think about your local area and the things you would like to do to help.

For number 6 you could turn some rubbish into something useful, plant bulbs, build a bug hotel or make bird feeders. Think about how you are helping the environment, and why this is a good thing to do.

TEAMWORK CHALLENGE AWARD

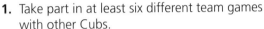

How to earn your award

For this award, you need to do these tasks over at least three months.

1. Take part in at least six different team games with other Cubs.
2. Show your leaders what you did to help your team, and how you were a good team player.
3. Give examples of two different types of teams, and roles in those teams.
4. Complete at least two teambuilding activities with other Cubs
5. Take part in at least two Pack forums or something similar, and make a contribution that will be positive for your Pack.

Top tips

Remember – a helpful team member is one who cooperates with the other members of the team, working together and communicating.

A Pack Forum is a chance for you to have your say. It could with the Pack, Six or just the Sixers, and you could talk about things like deciding on a programme activity or where to go on an outing.

TEAM LEADER CHALLENGE AWARD

How to earn your award

Once you have done the Teamwork Challenge Award, you can do your Team Leader Challenge Award. You earn your Team Leader Challenge Award by doing these tasks over at least three months.

1. Lead your Six in an activity or captain a team.
2. Help a new Cub to join in with the Pack meeting.
3. Teach another Cub a new skill.
4. Ask your Six or team what they want to do in Cubs, tell your leaders and help to make sure that it happens

Top tips

You have to complete this award to achieve your Chief Scout's Silver Award. It's a great one to do because:

- it gives you more of a challenge
- it gives you the chance to show your leadership skills
- it gives you the chance to be a leader if you haven't had the chance to be a Sixer yet.

PERSONAL CHALLENGE AWARD

How to earn your award

You need to complete two personal challenges that you agree with your leader. You should choose one of the challenges. Your leader will choose the other.

The challenges must be different to the ones that you did for your Beaver Personal Challenge Award.

Top tips

The challenges should be things that you find difficult but can complete with some effort and commitment. They can be to do with any part of your life, for example home, school or Cubs.

Here are some ideas for your personal challenge. You don't have to pick one of these; it should be something that is personal to you.

- Look after a new Cub for half a term.
- Talk about a topic you are interested in, with an adult you don't know very well.
- Bring the right equipment to Cubs every week for a term.
- Remember to brush your teeth twice a day for two weeks.

- Show good behaviour at Cubs for three weeks in a row.
- Try something new that you are a bit nervous about.
- Go to a District fun day and talk to some other Cubs you don't know.
- Try all of the food on Cub camp.
- Remember to feed your pet every morning for a week.
- Help to look after a sick or disabled friend or relative.

CHIEF SCOUT'S SILVER AWARD

This badge is the highest award you can get in Cubs. It shows that you have done your very best and made the most of your time. It might seem like a lot to do, but remember it'll be fun. And you'll be doing most of it with your friends at Cubs.

Your leader will make sure you get the chance to earn your Chief Scout's Silver Award.

How to earn your award

1. Earn six activity or staged activity badges of your choice. They could be badges you gain outside of your normal meetings or ones you've worked towards at meetings.

2. Finish the seven challenge awards. They are:
- Our World Challenge Award
- Our Skills Challenge Award
- Our Outdoors Challenge Award
- Our Adventure Challenge Award
- Teamwork Challenge Award
- Personal Challenge Award
- Team Leader Challenge Award.

Top tips

If you haven't finished the steps for the Chief Scout's Silver Award when you're ready to move on to Scouts, you can finish them during your first term in the Scout Troop.

When you become a Scout, you can wear your Chief Scout's Silver Award on your uniform until you earn your Chief Scout's Gold Award.

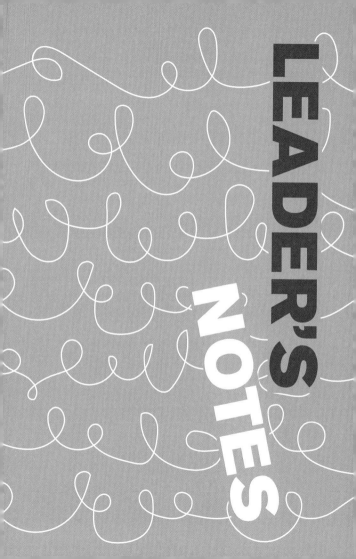

LEADER'S NOTES

BE SUPPORTIVE...

Notes for leaders and other adults supporting Cubs
This section is useful for any adult helping a Cub to work towards their badges. You might be a teacher, parent, carer or coach – everyone can play a role in helping Cubs achieve their goals.

Leaders should read this book in conjunction with Prepared, the leader manual, which contains important information about delivering the Cub programme as a whole.

You can also find badge requirements online at
scouts.org.uk

Cub badges

Badges and awards are an important part of the Cub programme. They provide vast array of activities that enrich Cubs' experiences and they're a great way of rewarding them. You'll probably notice that the challenges aren't easy. But in our experience Cubs enjoy working towards challenges. They're more likely to be motivated by achieving badges that take effort to complete.

Choosing badges

Cubs should attempt badges that meet their needs and interests, and are suitable for their abilities. Any activity should stretch them a little.

Wherever possible Cubs should be involved in choosing which badges they work towards, as part of their input into programme planning and review. More information about how young people can shape Scouting, including ideas on how to involve Cubs in generating ideas and reviewing their programme, can be found at
scouts.org.uk/youthinvolvement

Staged activities for Cubs

We know that some of the staged activities may seem very advanced for 8-10 year olds. It's usual for Cubs to start with stage 1 or 2 of these badges. These stages have been written with Beavers and Cubs mind.

We recognise, however, that some Cubs will have experienced certain activities from a young age. In this case they can start at whichever stage suits them best. It often depends on the hobbies they have outside of Scouting, such as swimming or music.

Staged activities offer more options to Cubs to develop their skills. Whichever level of badge a Cub is working towards, it should always be done safely and with their abilities in mind.

Adapting Badge and Award Requirements

Each young person who participates in the Programme, including badges and awards, should face a similar degree of challenge, and requirements can be adapted according to each young person's abilities.

The guiding principle throughout the Programme should be that young people are being challenged, while having fun. The requirements for badges provide a wide range of choice for young people, and most will be able to access the badges of their choice.

You may need to adjust the requirements to ensure that young people of different abilities all experience a similar level of challenge.

Adaptations made for young people with additional needs, medical conditions or disabilities should be aimed at improving access to the badge rather than reducing the challenge of its requirements or changing the focus. This may involve adapting some or all of the requirements and/or providing appropriate additional support.

In some instances, it may be appropriate to support the young people in your section to understand the adjustments, explaining that being fair doesn't always mean everyone doing exactly the same thing. In this situation, fair is about everyone being able to access the activity and experience a similar level of challenge. The nature of your conversation should take into consideration the age of the young people involved, the specific circumstances and the adaptations being made.

It is entirely up to the Leader how to adapt some or all of the badge or award requirements, in consultation with the young person and their parents or carers.

The things to consider are:
1. Whether the individual requirements can be adapted or whether they need to be replaced by an entirely different activity.
2. Whether to change the requirements for one young person or whether it is more appropriate to change them for the whole section to ensure the young person doesn't feel singled out.
3. Adapting some of the individual challenges into a team challenge, so that the young person

can use their individual strengths and abilities to achieve a team goal. Again, this avoids one Member being singled out.

4. When a badge or award is being undertaken as part of a group activity, it may be appropriate for all of the young people to be involved in the decision to alter the requirements. This will support the young people to better understand the reasons for the changes and be able to offer peer support.

For more information and tips about supporting young people with additional needs to fully participate in Scouting, see the Scouting for All section at **members.scouts.org.uk**

For further support please contact **info.centre@scouts.org.uk**

Disability Awareness

There is a Disability Awareness activity badge Cubs can go for. In lots of ways, it helps underpin some of the values Cub Scouts live by, when they make their Promise. It also helps Cubs understand how the whole group, including leaders, can support others to work towards their badges.

Leaders will find programme ideas that can help with this badge on Programmes Online.

You might also find these websites useful:

- Scope – **scope.org.uk**
- Paralympics – **paralympics.org.uk**
- Whizz-Kidz – **whizz-kidz.org.u**k
- Action on Hearing Loss (previously RNID) – **actiononhearingloss.org.uk**
- National Deaf Children's Society (NDCS) – **ndcs.org.uk**
- British Sign – **british-sign.co.uk**
- Sense – **sense.org.uk**
- Royal National Institute of Blind People (RNIB) – **rnib.org.uk**
- Guide Dogs – **guidedogs.org.uk**
- Goalball UK – **goalballuk.com**
- Omniglot (information about braille) – **omniglot.com**
- National Autistic Society – **autism.org.uk**
- Mencap – **mencap.org.uk**
- British Dyslexia Association – **bdadyslexia.org.uk**
- British Stammering Association – **stammering.org**
- Dyslexia Action – **dyselxiaaction.org.uk**
- Down Syndrome Association – **downs-syndrome.org.uk**
- Dyspraxia Foundation – **dyspraxiafoundation.org.uk**
- Tourettes Action – **tourettes-action.org.uk**

Delivering badges as part of the programme

If you're a leader, you might like to deliver Cub badges as part of the normal Pack programme. You may need to call on others who have specialist subject knowledge or equipment, and you're not expected to be able to deliver all of the badges in the Cubs section.

Consider asking people outside of your leadership team, such as parents, to help deliver badges. You could also think about visiting an external centre. It enables you to draw on people with a greater level of subject knowledge, which can be particularly helpful in delivering a broad range of different badges. You might even find that Cubs are inspired to hear from someone new, with specialist knowledge.

You can find programme material linking to many badges, particularly to the Challenge Awards, on Programmes Online at **scouts.org.uk/pol**

Achieving and awarding badges

You don't need a formal 'assessor' to sign that a Cub has completed a badge. Any relevant adult can confirm that the Cub has met the grade, such as an instructor, swimming coach, teacher or adult with knowledge of the subject. Leaders can then award the badge.
You might want to encourage Cubs to bring in things that they have done to achieve their badge, such as food they have cooked, or pictures of them doing a particular activity. If leaders talk to Cubs about what they did, they

can then make an informed decision about whether the Cub has done what's required to award the badge.

When to award badges

Once a Cub has achieved all that's required for a badge, you should award it as soon as possible. It keeps the achievement fresh in Cubs' minds. Most badges should be awarded at the end of a Pack meeting, but you may want to think about awarding some at a time and place that's special to the Cub. You could award a Nights Away badge while camping, or you could hold a special party for Cubs when they achieve their Chief Scout's Silver Award.

You can buy badges from your District Badge Secretary. If you are unsure who that is then ask your Group Scout leader or other leaders in your District.

Safety for leaders

Scouting should be delivered in a safe environment and some badges include activities that involve specific safety rules or guidance. We've added an icon, like the one above, to certain badges in this book. It highlights that there are specific safety rules to follow.

Whichever badge Cubs are involved in, always follow the safety advice provided in Prepared and make sure Cubs are supervised by adults with relevant skills.

What is community impact?

The Community Impact badge encourages Scouts to take practical action in the service of others, in order to create positive social change. It benefits the wider community as well as the young people taking part. Encourage Scouts to go for this badge and help them consider these questions:

1. Do you want to take action on issues affecting people in your local area, across the country or all across the world?

2. Is the action you want to take relevant to the community you're trying to help? Or is it trying to fix a problem that doesn't exist?

3. Will it genuinely change the lives of others, or is it just a nice thing to do?

4. Will the action you want to take genuinely develop you as a person? Or is it actually quite boring, mundane and not very much fun?

Identifying need

Social issues can affect different people in different ways. Young people will face different problems from older people. Those living in the countryside will have different challenges from those who live in a city centre. Social issues in Scotland are very different from those in Tibet.

This requirement is about knowing what issues are relevant to the people you are trying to help. Young people should ask themselves:

1. Who in our chosen community will be an expert in the issues and challenges people face or are passionate about?
2. Are there other sources of research or information we can use to identify issues?
3. What issues do we care about?

Planning action

Community impact is about creating positive social change, so Scouts must be clear on what exactly they want to change before deciding on what practical action to take. You should help young people to ask themselves, in this order:

1. What is the problem they are trying to fix?
2. What needs to change to fix that problem?
3. What can we actually do to make that change?

Learning and continuing to make change

Community impact should develop the young person taking part, so your projects should have some kind of learning outcome. Young people should be given space to reflect and talk about what they have learned.

1. What have they learned about the issue they took action on?
2. What skills have they learned?
3. How have their values and attitudes developed?

The project should also contribute to social change, and that is unlikely to happen in a short space of time. So once they reach a stage where they consider their project finished, you should support young people to think further.

1. How could they improve their Community Impact project so that it reaches more people and makes a bigger impact?
2. How could they involve more people in their project?
3. Would they consider participating in a community impact project run by another organisation or group on the same or different issues?

Celebrating the work and inspiring others

Social change happens when others are inspired to take action. You should support young people to reach and inspire more people who can take action on their chosen issue. You could do this through:

- interacting with local media
- presenting to relevant groups of people such as local business, decision makers and other community groups
- interacting with other non-Scouting youth groups, such as schools, youth clubs and sports teams
- speaking to their own families, other Scout groups and sections.

LEADER'S NOTES

Staying safe online

The Digital Citizen and Digital Maker staged activity badges may involve performing some tasks online, and finding out about social networking. Before Cubs take part in these activities, you'll want to talk through a few safety rules first.

Check that Cubs understand that staying safe involves:

- using passwords to protect their computer and accounts, not using the same password or login for every account, and thinking about whether to use the auto remember function
- using trusted software
- not downloading things they are not sure about
- knowing what to do if they get an alert from anti-virus software
- recognising when they should ask an adult they trust before they visit a particular website
- understanding that some websites and software have age restrictions
- starting to assess whether the information they find on a website is true or reliable
- recognising the kind of information that is private (like their address and phone number) and that they should never give it out over the internet
- understanding that they are communicating with real people when they use email
- that emails should be clear and written with a respectful tone

- knowing who to report an issue to if they feel uncomfortable online, such as CEOP, a parent or leader.
- An online game called Stay Safe Online is available for Cubs. For more information, visit **digitalskills.scouts.org.uk**

Social networking

Examples of social networking sites that are suitable for the Cubs (8-10) age group include:
- Kibooku (6-13)
- Moshi Monsters (6-12)
- YourSphere (6-17)
- Skooville (6-14)
- ScuttlePad (6-11)
- SuperClubsPLUS (6-12)
- Club Penguin (6-14).

Social networking sites like Facebook, Flickr and Google+ are not suitable for Cubs, as they have an age limit of 13 years and over. You can find useful information and resources to help you talk about online safety with young people at:
- South West Grid for Learning **swgfl.org.uk**
- CEOP's online safety site **thinkuknow.co.uk**
- Digizen, digital awareness site **digizen.org**
- Childnet's 'Know it all online' safety advice **childnet.com/resources/kia**

- Digital Disruption online literacy skills
  digitaldisruption.co.uk

For more guidance and help organising any of the activities listed in this book, visit **scouts.org.uk/a-z**

NOTES

NOTES

NOTES